Sooty

Written by Shelley Jones
Photography by Michael Curtain

sundance®
A Haights Cross Communications ☀® Company

This is my cat Sooty.
It's my job to take care of her.

Sometimes she does
bad things.

Every morning, she jumps
on my mom's bed.
I tell her not to,
but she still does it.

3

Two birds live in our backyard.
Sooty shouldn't chase them,
but she does.

The birds fly away when they see Sooty.

This is Sooty's bell.
The bell hangs on the back door.

Sooty rings the bell
when she wants to come inside.
I open the door for her
when the bell rings.

It's my job to feed Sooty.
Sooty likes to eat a lot.
She eats crunchy cat food,
and she drinks lots of water.

Sooty likes to play games.

She likes to crawl inside a paper bag.
Sometimes she hides in it
and jumps out at me.

I think she looks funny
with her head in a paper bag.

Sooty is a very clean cat.
She licks her fur to keep it clean.

Sooty has her own brush.

She likes to play with her brush,
but she doesn't like it very much
when I brush her.

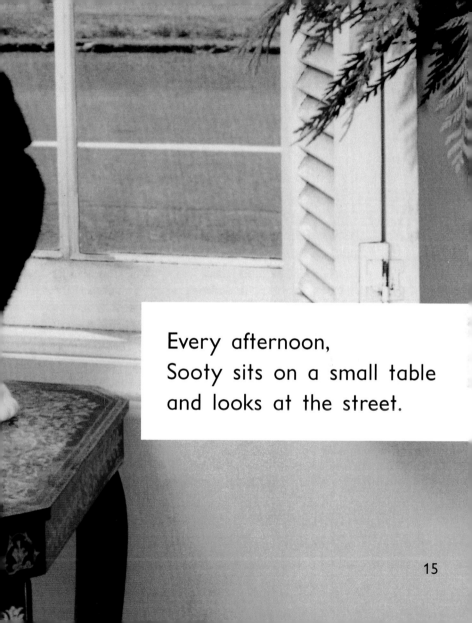

Every afternoon,
Sooty sits on a small table
and looks at the street.

Sooty waits at the window
until I come home from school.
I love my cat Sooty!